AMORISCO

Khaled Mattawa

AUSABLE PRESS
2008

Cover art: "Bio gestation" by Yamou, 2005
Oil on canvas, 57" x 44.20"

Author photo: Amanda Abel
Design and composition by Ausable Press
The type is Bembo with Bembo Titling.
Cover design by Rebecca Soderholm

Published by
Ausable Press
1026 Hurricane Road
Keene, NY 12942
www.ausablepress.org

Distributed to the trade by
Consortium Book Sales & Distribution
34 Thirteenth Avenue NE, Suite 101
Minneapolis, MN 55413-1007
(612) 746-2600
Order FAX: (800) 351-5073
Orders: (800) 283-3572

The acknowledgements appear on page 77 and constitute a
continuation of the copyright page.

Library of Congress Cataloging-in-Publication Data

Mattawa, Khaled.
Amorisco : poems / by Khaled Mattawa. —1st ed.
p. cm.
ISBN 978-1-931337-44-1 (pbk. : alk. paper)
I. Title

PS3563.A8387A83 2008
811'.54—dc22
2008032811

For Reem and Salma:

Of course, their voices rise
when lies are exchanged,
but are they telling truth
in the whispering
that never seems to end . . .
                          —Abu al-Ala al-Maari

ALSO BY KHALED MATTAWA

Poetry:

Zodiac of Echoes, Ausable Press, 2003

Ismailia Eclipse, The Sheep Meadow Press, 1995

Translations:

Iman Mersal, *These Are Not Oranges, My Love*
The Sheep Meadow Press, 2008

Joumana Haddad, *Invitation to a Secret Feast*
(editor) Tupulo Press, 2008

Maram Al-Massri, *A Red Cherry on a White-Tile Floor*
Bloodaxe Press (U.K.), 2004; Copper Canyon Press, 2007

Fadhil Al-Azzawi, *Miracle Maker*
BOA Editions, 2004

Saadi Youssef, *Without an Alphabet, Without a Face: Selected Poems*
Graywolf Press, 2002

Fadhil Al-Azzawi, *In Every Wall a Joseph Is Weeping*
Quarterly Review of Literature, 1997

Hatif Janabi, *Questions and Their Retinue: Selected Poems*
University of Arkansas Press, 1996

Anthologies:

Dinarzad's Children: Anthology of Contemporary Arab American Fiction
(co-editor), University of Arkansas Press, 2004

Post Gibran: New Arab American Writing (co-editor)
Syracuse University Press, 1999

AMORISCO

I.

AGAINST ETHER

With my certainties, I assemble the elements.

A burned suit,   the earth's gloved hand
                     a book made of petals.

Daylight's answer evaporates before our eyes.

Seek out another heart, another whistle from a train.

Night remains the gist of the story.

The people of my country   a galaxy of winter lies.

                    ❧

We burst through dirt like wild artichokes.
We were water from a bucket from which the family horse drank,
          a fugue   a mirror learning to talk.

In our stories, the king of rain and the princess of stone
share a grave inside a flame
                         reddened by the blood of exile
or the blood of an ox.

And when the story pauses
our life becomes an octopus waving its flags.

                    ❧

There was a ship behind a scaffolding
and a wrecked train.

Every day a vision of the future walked to the river
and threw away a bag of bones.
Horror was clay we tore off the air.
These are the shapes we made:

A man polishes his shoes preparing to go to mass. The shoes are
polished already, his wife's work, but this is a ritual he enjoys and
she endures. Let this happen where the trees are gnarled witches:
pomegranates, mulberries, eucalyptus, white boulders half-buried in
red dirt.

So you call your mother and she asks for wool socks and you buy
her a dozen. Please come with me to look through the keyhole. Your
father is standing in the tub. Old age makes him stagger and your
mother is helping him bathe. She towels him dry then slaps a bit
of cologne on his face.

I can no longer speak of waterwheels, each spin a bucketful.
The sun crosses the pool from end to end—
and the mist rising from bean fields—bird calls and wind-chimes,
snakes of light twist at the end of every road.

O Mother
your feet, the years of fieldwork like tree rings grooved in cracked
heels.

I can no longer speak of the distances the body must travel to speak
to itself.

Seek out another alphabet
                         a new vowel to house your edges
                         a way to rename your days.
           Count the hours of the half-lives to come.
           Photograph the faces
                         open-mouthed   eyes closed.
           Ride the highways of hand-to-mouth
                         one shoulder pushing billions of wheels.
           A room housing dormant despairs
                         a classroom   a jail
                         the accountants learning a new map.
           The elderly who live and live
                         and live and live
                         the dead born young flashing chains.

                    ❧

Beyond the fence, rain falls where the soft air ends. Someone walks into
the downpour, time where destinations blur and begin to compose,
the foghorn blaring unscored.

                    ❧

In his farm my father grows what the seasons let him.

This is how he plants his crops:

He takes off his hat
and lets the rain talk to him.
He holds a fistful of dirt
and pleads with it.

CHILDHOOD FRIDAYS

The mornings tormented me.
Why are you smiling?

The streets turned quiet, the stores
pulled down their serrated iron doors.

Prayers swirled in the air like vines
choking the neighborhood.

Perhaps I loved Thursdays too much—how
they fooled me into dreaming a different life.

Why are you still smiling at me?

How could I have known
that God made the world in six days,

and on the seventh
played dead.

BEFORE HURON

How does it know to set so evenly—
angels in silver jumpsuits surveying
with milky wings, steamrollers

powered by what grace, what divine
fingerwork? Or was it the sweet taste
of apple in the Mother's mouth,

her sweet saliva of rain? How my mother
fretted to catch it in barrels, in tubs,
how she scrubbed the flat roof, let

the first rain mop it and it flowed in spigots,
a faint shadow of our valley's copper dust,
then she'd sigh later at the waste,

the waste! sheets of it clear and gleaming,
a shade found in pearls and salt, sliding
then trickling in rivulets into a sewer hole.

Why would the wind not bite its teeth
into it, making potholes like everything
human? Is the horizon it makes

unblemished a sign, a phantom of justice
appearing and disappearing
disappointing the young prophet,

the Canaanite who watched a star wane
then burn, flooding the horizon with its
flesh-colored wax, a mirror bloat like a

balloon then starve itself to a desiccated
feather of stone, feather of gray peacock
lighter than dawnlight held in your palm?

CORPUS CHRISTI

Your head buzzing with Lorca, flashbacks
of Almodovar drowning scenes—still,
I don't know why you went to Spain.
An archeological dig or business school?
Someone sent white roses, no note. In the yard,
I aimed the shotgun, then a drizzle of petals,
snow, cocaine. Your cat eats in the same corner; now
catches her own squirrels. There's a book about you,
all the little scandals you bragged about at parties—
the Polaroids of you and the mayor and his wife
sprawled nude on the traffic court bench.
Or your two trained pigs squealing the National Anthem
while you romped in a playground sand box.
I told them nothing about the baby iguanas
your father stole from the zoo, greased and baked,
nothing about the tufts of hair we yanked off
old ladies we abducted for ransom, or the peanut butter
jars filled with gnashed teeth. The last time
you called, the line was static and your voice
felt like hydrogen peroxide in my ear.
I sent 22 telegrams and you didn't answer. Now,
I drive to Lubbock on weekends. I think of you
among beat-up cars and broken glass, among
sawed-off guitars and hollow drums.
I think of the burlap jacket you made me,
the cheese cloth dresses you wore,
your mother's ashes, how you fed some
to your violets then poured the rest inside
a peppershaker in Houston's Hard Rock Café.
And the live wire across the street!
Birds tipped it for landing, the shock jerking them

back up, their screams short shrill gargles, then
on the sidewalk—two charred halves, the pile
of them you collected in the rear porch,
how stray dogs came barking at night,
how I clubbed two raccoons that broke the screen
and one left a scar on my calf. Love,
why can't we lie again on the sand,
chunks of cauliflower between our toes,
sunbathers gawking at us like they've always done,
and we weeping for their sake, because no one else would,
not the sky that's been clear for two years,
or the puny mist rising from the river, or the sea
doddering like a sloth? Let's leave now
and drive to the shady side of a plaza, watch
Mexican children run between gray and bronze,
fade in and out of a sun-scorched dream.

ADOLESCENCE OF BURNT HANDS

Suddenly I found my sorrow among
strange trees, on dusty squares.
I thought yes,
yes,

I knew it had to come.
I had seen it on men's faces.
But too early, too soon.
I said,

"Sorrow of the distant Mother,
Ghosts of schoolyard friends,
Father broken backbone,
I am too young to live without anger."

Then everywhere I went
it was the valley of God's absence,
the forest of the cold bosom,
the deserts where children raised children.

And I cradled my flame.

HEARTSONG

A bird sings from the tree. The birds sing
sending waves of desire and I stand on my roof
waiting for a randomness to storm my days. I stand
on my roof filled with the longing that sings its way
out of the bird. I am afraid that my call will break me,
that the cry blocked by my tongue will pronounce me mad.
O bird mad with longing, O balancing bar,
tight rope, monkey grunting from a roof. Fortunate bird.
I stand on my roof and wave centuries of desire.
I am the Bedouin pondering the abandoned campsite,
licking the ashes of the night fire; the American walking,
walking miles of dresses, blouses, and skirts filling them
with infinite lovers, the mystic feeling the pull swirling
in his chest, a desert of purpose expanding and burning
and yellowing every shade of green. And I stand on my roof.
And I say come like a stranger, like a feather
falling on an old woman's shoulder, like a hawk
that comes to feed from her hands, come like a mystery,
like sunlight rain, a blessing, a bus falling off a bridge,
come like a deserting soldier, a murderer chased by law,
like a girl prostitute escaping her pimp, come like a lost horse,
like a dog dying of thirst, come love, come ragged
and melancholy like the last day on earth, come like a sigh
from a sick man, come like a whisper, like a bump on the road,
like a flood, a dam breaking, turbines falling from the sky,
come love like the stench of a swamp, a barrage of light
filling a blind girl's eye, come like a memory convulsing
the body into sobs, like a carcass floating on a stream,
come like a vision, come love like a crushing need,
come like an afterthought. Heart song. Heart song.
The pole smashes and the live wires yellow streaks

on the lush grass. Come look and let me wonder. Someone.
So many. The sounds of footsteps, horses and cars.
Come look and let me wonder. I stand on my roof
echoing the bird's song: Do not sleep. Do not sleep now
that you have housed your longing within the pain of words.

THE OLD HOUSE WITH THEE

In my dreams a promise of water, relief drifts like a log.

The sink where I washed my face.

Here, rage slipped its oily hands into me. A knife to my brother, imagining spilled guts.

I am awake now.

Some day I will bring hammers and begin the destruction,

the canvas streaked with crimson songs, weddings, smoke rising from the blind musicians' clarinets.

The neighborhood informant snooping around.

And here my mother's visitors sat.

One neighbor wept to her own story, a beating, a summer in Alexandria.

Sweat and the dancing thighs' jelly shake.

Some day, a bulldozer smashing through walls.

᠁

A phantom may simply claim the old house, in the name of justice.

The testicles he electrocuted, the nails he pulled off the disappeared, will be his proofs.

Come to me my patched dreams and shield me.

Mother, and I, her scribe who knew when to drop his pen and leave.

Sold now.

Another room, another floor. Plant a plum tree where the date palm stood.

❧

Years ago, not far from sirens and street-corner prostitutes, I meddle with the window, the screen fragile, but stubborn-gnarled.

I jump in certain the neighbors will not call the police.

We smoke a cigarette, that room with orange walls and deep blue velvet curtains. The squalor, the estrangement. She dozing on my arm.

Mobile, Alabama, the first sleep of love.

❧

I walk the old house, after many stops, many stamps, and the dry air of hotel rooms.

There's beauty in that avowal, the future a washline, the white sheets stiff with starch, the disinfected blankets' metallic reek.

On television, Post-Wall porn, the same couple, sweet nothings dubbed in Turkish, Italian, Portuguese.

You didn't care to know how sunrise streamed through the south-facing window. How the shadows of birds flitted across the sun-drenched bed and walls.

The porn couple smoke a cigarette, and an old world visits the room, a breeze, a gust from the AC vent.

I am now in the no–house–at–all.

❧

The house we dreamed of, a double dream.

Your seascapes and lighthouses and my impossible abode.

To you, they said nothing, those windblown branches brushing against the roof.

What made me see imagination going slack in its harness?

The sofa here?

The never-ending welcome, the staying put, a candle in your hand.

Whose mother will hang on which wall?

Did you just say abode?

❧

Eavesdropping, that's where I'd heard that the neighbor's husband had spent a month barhopping in Alexandria. Sweat and the dancing thighs. Venereal disease.

I walk the old house.

Onward until self-possession breaks into our lives.

Yesterday, two decades since Mobile.

❧

I kick at broken stones, wipe dust off my forehead.

A month or two, concrete columns rising, new trees casting shadows on the street.

I help them bring in furniture, hand them the keys.

And for years, I visit unannounced, see them languid in their nightclothes or huddled by a kerosene heater.

They show me a girl's name etched on a closet door, a loose tile on the flat roof for a pack of cigarettes I hid.

The neighborhood informant, a wandering soul snooping around.

IN PRAISE OF PRAISE

To give what is deserved, to polish
what had never dimmed or been allowed
to slip away from luster, to crawl deep
into memory, to step into the cellar
and wipe with one's sleeve
what must fight off reclamation,
the spider web, the tight acidic work
of the dirt's slow engine,
to continue in psalm lest the sky fall
upon its lanterns, to rescue a lost comet
drifting toward the mind's carbon,
to give oneself to the rescue, to remind,
for remembrance is the first breath of faith,
for what we are remains flesh, and that is why
the tongue must bolster what no echo can haul.
Praise praise—I throw myself into your orbit
chanting, chanting, and when I pause,
you'll know your horizon's edge.
Praise that good, even when misidentified,
mislabeled, misguided can be wrought.
Praise the surrender, the denial,
the idea that something is worth saving
that we can seek what can save us.

BUSTER

We call out to the night sky, the heart's compass falters,
beseech the eye to witness us through unmapped days.
I know that inside my eye there's a sky swirling.
I know too that the night is an eye gazing at us, a sea on which the
      flotsam of sympathy floats.
I call until there is no more call, then slowly feel the hollow as
      something gored,
a pair of parentheses filling in with all that whizzes past.
But the dream has no dream in it,
the same refraction sounding from the cold air,
a semblance of a thought shot out onto the sunlight drizzling through
      leaves
received now when called upon like a trip to the grocery store to buy
      my nocturnal cigar.
Times when I look into my own eyes as if staring at an eclipse, the
      soul's retina like a spider web collapsing, thwacked by a cat's paw.

I know this sounds pathetic.
I know it proves all the rumors.
When I look into his eyes he sometimes squints and slowly closes
them telling me he's
              content and I should leave him alone.
Sometimes he scrunches his hind legs telling me his kidneys are
      failing him,
but he doesn't know that he's telling me anything
or that he has kidneys to begin with.
He doesn't know that I think he thinks I can solve his problems,
doesn't know that he thinks at all,
or that right now I'm thinking I need to change his diet, and that a
      visit to the vet might help.
He doesn't know that I think it's too early for him to suffer

and doesn't know that that last thought saddens me.
Years ago I too had theories
and what remains of my asking
knots and tangles in another sphere, grows and grows its own heart,
        and what was inculcated—
a lover who sighed as her mother's mother sighed at the same things—
        continues to flinch at stimuli.
"The heart, the heart," we say "not mine, almost theirs, and no one's."
We dream of it cracking out of its shell, soaring into oblivion,
as in the dream of cold fusion, an element coming into being of its
        own accord,
a dream of cold comfort
that splutters in the dark, warm milk of our chests.

As soon as I get out of the car, he meows.
I say luvvy, luvvy, luvvy.   He meows.
Say you're the best trapeze artist in China.
O beautiful pimp!
O island princess with a ruby in her belly-button,
and I when I open the door, he darts to the kitchen and waits at his
        bowl.
Sometimes he looks at me startled,
widens the lids of his eyes, and shrinks his pupils as if a flashlight has
        been put right at his face.
I'd point to food, water, the litter box, the door,
but he holds that look,
or it holds him and me in it.
Then he walks off,
the tabby sunset of his grace.

Would I have broached the subject had I been a different accident?
After all we did pick him up from the animal shelter, but what drew
        us to him?
Something in us twined, and gravitating outward,
something telling us that the basis (even) of our love for each other—

she and love's gray matter—
each of the cats in their cages loud with their idiosyncrasies—
is like a fruit resting atop a modula oblongata of forgiveness.
What was timeless in our action without an era to give it that designation?
To what end this unstoppable calculus?
Will it find us a lineage to explain your you, my I,
a psychic manna towards which we reach simultaneously: Here love,
          have a taste?

The dream in the dream is of continuity not the soft landing of
          accomplishment, the sickening desire for home.
Oh poetry, singing a nursery rhyme in the no-home of home.
Oh poetry, how much you've acknowledged, neither lopping off the
          prisoner's head nor releasing him.
How long will you remain an expression of helplessness,
how many times will you gaze into a cat's eye and say "this too will pass"?

Still, I know how my heart is beating.
I know what keeps me from sleeping,
from waking.
A color,
a kind of climate,
an inherent melody as if my bones were the flutes playing it.
How long can I keep defying it?
How come I've not found a way to shield myself from it?
I know too that there is a way to think of it as contagion, a common
          catharsis.

But dear Christopher Smart, isn't such a pleasure also an old, old thing?
Notice how it kicks in right after waking,
how it even interrupts sleep, jostling with its cousin fear.
Is that why you projected your mania on everything you saw,
kneeling in the middle of a street, or in a tavern, seeing every act a
          prayer?

Wasn't the mere notice of things acknowledgement enough?
The prayer tossing the dark thought into the cosmos
hoping it would never drift back.

His name is Buster and he busts what he can.
For this is more than a lifetime's worth of words and what they shake
        off from the branches or gather from waves, mist, and foam.
For he has brought to me the time of my living.
For in my weakness I'm now a specimen of the majority.
For I've almost given up on wishing upon myself the prestige of an
        interesting pathology.
For he has slept beside me like a brother.
For he once brought me the lower half of a squirrel, gutted and clean.

II.

PASTORAL

We talk like strangers.
This is how
we bring back

that first seduction.
You tell a story.
Your face wears

an old diffidence.
And because your story
is new to me,

I become new
to you. You pause
between sentences,

surprised by
what you tell,
surprised

at the stranger
that I am to you.
When your story ends,

new words—their ink
glistening still—
are inscribed

over the old.
Estranged, we
seek each other,

behold our
selves meeting
among the crowds

we have become.

RAIN-PUDDLE BIRDS BATHE AT DUSK

Their feet fastforward, a current
runs through their bodies
                    shaking the water off.

You are here working and I am disbelieving,
weighing the day's air.

Daylight, leaves, shapes projected
shapes distorted,
                    a hand nudges the world.

You turned to look.
I had already left the room.

An old idea emerging, a cause
out of shaving cream and shampoo foam

(It's like a face,
sometimes there is little to love)

and new inventions, a life on the make:

Fame, success
old age without loneliness
and other deferred schemes.

❧

What I know I cannot stir.
Forgetfulness and stars that fade

into disappointments, reminiscences
held by a pat on the back, short embrace.

Some walk without legs.
Some split in two, lean and crutch

on stone minutes and hours of talk.
No shafts of light, no betrayals in the dust.

You, you, warming milk bereft of words,
with small mirrors assembling self.

What was it?

A New Year's Eve on the road,
                    an awkward dance?

A light in the hall, a small moonbeam,
you falling, falling asleep, not letting go,

and triumphs of sighs, a blanket soaked
in sweat.

The nothing that was nothing
                            is itself again,
and that which was lost
                    lost again,
the sound of my footsteps,
                    the world's roar.

EARLY ADULTHOOD

We made fires, outlined the conspiracies.
The scent of smoke lingered on our hands.

Straggling summer clouds, like newsless travelers,
gave the century the same name others gave theirs.

Some of us sent prayers skyward. Some slumped
in chairs, others sat up, their backs taut.

Does it matter who of these I was then
when under a clear sky all options were justified?

Yes, I thought of what I'd promised you.
But who was I then, or should I say what am I

in that place, or anywhere
and why, O why, does it keep changing?

Another language, another betrayal. The star
that once bloodied my grasp, a pinch of red dust.

THE VIOLET BENDS TO THE STUBBLE
SKIRTING IT

and the cat's head follows the arc of a sparrow's flight.
When you asked me "Are you sure you want to go?"
I said "no," and obeyed what I will never be able to name.
When I call out to you now
I still have to pause before calling her name,
and for endearments I have failed to tell you
anything other than what I've whispered to her.

But that's not why I'm not in love.

Once when I was ten I saw a neighbor
step out into a cold afternoon, shirtless.
He stood in front of his house, raised his arms
and yelled a triumphant cry. And as if to terrorize me
he let out a loud laugh.
He was the neighborhood "drinker"
reputed to sell the "grappa" he made in his garage.

Why am I telling you this
when all I want to say is that I'm not in love?

I sensed my terror and swaddled it in the coat
wrapped around me. But what am I holding now
as I kiss you, as I caress your soft arms,
your hands fragile like sparrows
in my palms.

These must be among the satisfactions that lie beyond our reach, the
ones we recognize and crave and from which we eventually recoil.

Once in a friend's garden I had tea with three men. The youngest among them spoke about an upcoming nephew's marriage they'd recently arranged. He complimented the choice of bride and the new in-laws as being 'like us', meaning modest, virtuous, reputable, but so low-key that a scandal would not do them irreparable harm. How can I describe that man's glee, his eyes two small flames in the afternoon turning dusk? For he has become a special kind of elder, young enough to facilitate a match and respected enough to object and be heard. How distant I felt from these men, their whole business reeking of senseless, mummified traditions!

A breeze blows and the stubble sends the violet
a ruffian salute. The violet is unmoved,
but if you'd look closer it'd be easy to imagine
a tingling falling from its pistil to its thinnest root.
The cat watches like a Mafioso
with a developed taste for abstract art.

Sometimes I sit next to my mother in the large living room, and I
        can tell she is not with me at all,
thinking of my father perhaps, or more likely thinking of her own
        death.
The last time we both saw him alive she told me "it's as if he'd crawled
        out of a grave."
So many close calls had left us calloused.
The so-much-still-to-do, the rug of one's life too far undone.
She sits there as if I am a distant light in her rear view mirror.
But I have nowhere to go, having come from so far away to be with her
and having nothing to do there but to be her son.
So I ask her to tell a story

and she takes my lead as if she'd picked up a hitchhiker, glad for
        company and the purpose her companion gives her.

Don't ask me what I'll do when that old woman dies. I can't bear
        the thought.

I think she thinks my father is now where he wants to be,
doing what he liked to do most,
which was work, and to fret about work,
seeking accolades he'd not gotten in earthly life,
and never ever crying over spilt milk.

Sometimes, I'd like to think, that when she's deep in her telling, the
        hitchhiker she picks up bears the face of a man she loves,
and there they ride away into the dawn.

None of this has anything to do with you,
none of this has anything to do with not wanting to be in love.

When the drinker's wife knocked on our door one night,
my father answered.
He heard the woman out, but only offered to take her to the police.
Other neighbors took her in,
and because she was a foreigner, and because I knew what that meant
        even then,
I felt ashamed for her.
I never asked my father why he'd been so ungenerous because I
        thought one day I'd understand.

I still don't understand.

The man I spoke of earlier, whose life was beginning to ripen, imagine
him the same night he was engaged in matchmaking returning home
to the usual clutter of toys, the older boy not letting his younger
brother have his turn at the PlayStation, the toddler whimpering

hanging on to his mother's dress, but she's cooking and has no time to carry him. She shouts from inside the kitchen at her daughter, who has found a fondness for the telephone, to pick up her baby brother and wash his face and take him to bed, but the girl pretends she hasn't heard, and her mother shouts again, this time threatening to smack her. It's at this moment that the man enters his house, and he is quickly aware that his girl is not being "a good older daughter," aware too that she's reached puberty, which now makes him think that he needs to tell her mother that the girl must dress differently, no more jeans or tight shirts, and he's also aware that she's a pretty girl, and in a few years someone will come and ask for her hand. Before saying hello he commands the girl to go to the kitchen and pick up the toddler, he turns to the boys and asks if they've done their homework, and enters the kitchen—his wife has never looked more beautiful to him, and he has never been happier and suspects he may never be this happy again.

Am I telling you about this man because it will not surprise you
that tragedy cannot slam her brakes in time,
that change leads us through entrances to the self that keep shrinking?
Yes, it's a different story, one that has nothing to do with not being
    in love.

When my father died,
I felt emboldened with resolve,
my heart guided by a forgiving sense of clarity.
It was an exhilarating feeling.
I was strangely in love with the world.
A few months later he began to reel me in, and I lay at his feet
    floundering.
He'd appear before me in the bed I saw him die in,
and as if on cue I'd begin to interrogate myself in his presence.
I could never tell if he wanted to forgive or be forgiven.
Even in sleep I rocked to his brutal wavering.

Listen, what can I weave when my hands keep slipping,
when the walls I reach for bend to my touch?

I think I hear a tune plucked on oedipal chords.
I think I hear Hamlet dithering in his old age.
Must be the mood I'm in.

How else to brace you in your blooming, violet rising
among stubble in parched fields?
That man is now a wet sparrow in the cold rain of widowhood,
his children more fragile than your hands,
and you open and ready, wanting to love your life,
to be surprised by your love for it,
leaning down on me, your weight doubled with joy,
tripled with a ghost of despair.
I bend,
and I'm easily seducible,
and you rise,
and you climb to place another brick
in the wall of your happy fortress.

Go ahead, I'll be your ladder again.
This, you know, can go on for the rest of our lives.
But I'm not going anywhere.
I'm not in love.

WHICH

There is a prayer named after it,
the cushion,
                    the fork in the road.
A clarinet this time, the trombones
straggle in
            shuffling their feet.
There is a WHO in it.
The hard place.
                        The ghoul.
                The slitter of throats.
Afterwards
she turned   pale
            a mouse
emerging from the flour sack.
Have mercy on yourself,
                    that is the way
of the faith I know,
                    the light
from the swimming pool shining
into the apartment,
                    the water
a piece of sky; the leaves floating over it
                    were birds.
You say, what are you going to do?
I ask you, what do you think?
The rock
            between the shallots
and the garlic shoots.
There is   an onion   in it,
and a way to keep out of the cold.

The psychic

      you went to see,
the crowds   waiting   to be told.
The lines in my palm.

       The soft place.
Regret in the afternoon.

        A gesture
in the morning. Your hand
brushing it

     off.

THE IN-BETWEEN

Afternoons contemplating the unspeakable
in the city of jewels, the city
of massacred jewelers, contemplating
the pillow, the body that suffers
and radiates its suffering. Tonight

the Black Forest sends her slugs
crawling all over the hospital pavements.
It's awkward not to kill them,
not to recognize the forest's bounty,
not to see the sacrifice
in its thoughtless offering.

Outside in the smoking area
the young and burdened chat football
or pace contemplating euthanasia,
brothers, sisters in phone booths saying
"you must do your part, I'm tired,
I've done the best I can."

No one prays, the clippings on the walls,
in Luther's words drone,
a monopoly silencing that longing.

I don't want either side of this river.
I don't want my life to be the ferry
bridging its banks. Other shadows lure me,
new lives to bring into the afternoons
that course through me like fast trains
shaking beams, rattling rafters,
other stories to nudge into their telling.

Not quietude, only the strange respite
in the free fall, the way skydivers
clasp hands and form a circle
as if they'll hang there forever.
Some days the parachute clicks like
an empty gun, and one either wastes
the moment in epithets and panic or

lets go into the swiftness,
the marvel now clasping shut,
my birth a flash of lightning,
this blooming stain a roll of thunder.
But the parachute catches; it rarely fails,
the body jolted back up, then the fall
slow and unnatural.

Forgive me if I've raised your hopes
having praised the in-between so often.
The suffering body now resumes
its sluggish pace, demanding to be
lifted into some brief comfort,
its moans quieter, less frequent,
the patient well enough to stand
to be washed, doused with cologne.

I stare into the light, the distance,
the low mountains and their river
as they pull at the spool of my days
and with every breath, a thread
of farewell inching further.

BEDTIME READING FOR
THE UNBORN CHILD

Long after the sun falls into the sea
and twilight slips off the horizon like a velvet sheet
and the air gets soaked in blackness;
long after clouds hover above like boulders
and stars crawl up and stud the sky;
long after bodies tangle, dance, and falter
and fatigue blows in and bends them
and sleep unloads its dreams and kneads them
and sleepers dive into the rivers inside them,
a girl unlatches a window,
walks shoeless into a forest,
her dark hair a flag rippling in darkness.

She walks into woods, her feet light-stepping
through puddles, over hard packed dirt,
through grassy hills, over sticks and pebbles
over sand soaked in day, stones sun-sizzled
over lakes and frigid streams
through dim cobbled streets
darkened squares and dusty pastures.
She runs from nothing, runs to nothing,
beyond pain, beyond graveyards and clearings.
In the dark the eyes of startled creatures
gleam like a herd of candles.
They scatter and give night its meaning.

What echo of a bell lulled her
what spirit, what scent of a word
whose storm wrote her

what banks fell to drown her
which blood star
which thread of water
which trickle of light
whose heart being launched
whose floating soul seduced her
what promise did it make her
whose memory burned her
whose prayer did she run to answer
whose help, what sorrow clot
what pain dammed inside her
what wall must she rebuild now
whose treasure beckons her
who spread ivy like a veil to blind her?
Daybreak lies chained to a blue wall
from which the stars drop
and lose all meaning.

She runs past villages that lost their names
roads that lost their destinations
seas that lost their compasses and sailors
rivers that lost their marshlands and travelers
houses that lost their sleepers and criers
trees that lost their songs and shadows
gardens that lost their violets and benches
valleys that lost their worms and farmers
mountains that lost their prophets and marauders
temples that lost their sinners and spires
lightning that lost its silver and wires
chimeras that lost their bridges
minotaurs that lost their fountains.
Crescent moons hover above her,
ancient white feathers, birdless, wingless
lost to their own meaning.

Music rises out of her vision.
It stands, a wall covered with silver mosses.
A clarinet sounds a wounded mare,
violins women who lost their children.
Flutes blow their hot dry breezes.
Drums chuckle the earth's ceaseless laughter.
Pianos are mumbling sorcerers
calling spirits and powers.
Cellos chew on the sounds of thunder.
Dulcimers skip about on crutches.
Dance floors flash their knives
daring their dancers.
Words mill about the streets like orphans.
Then a lute begins groaning
and dawn loses its meaning.

Night girl, night girl
your book is full now.
You have drawn all the pictures.
You have seen many weepers.
Stars held your sky in place and moons
floated on your lakes and washed them.
When a bird sings
when dewed branches tilt sunlight into eyes
when curtains are soaked with light
when mirrors drown in shadows,
take your day to the shore, my child.
Put out the words that fired your waking,
scatter them on the sand like seeds,
then with your feet gently tap them,
and let the bright waves
receive your meaning.

REDRESS

The relative who wronged you
you've already mistreated twice.
The friend who betrayed you—
and whom you betrayed—you've reconciled
since then, many kisses on the cheek.

The ex-lover who's badmouthed you
and you've badmouthed in return—
how blissful it'd be to be together again,
tracing scars you left on each other,
regret fueling your passionate sex.

This last thought pleases you as
you search for the proper pan,
the newly sharpened knife
that will slice up tonight's meal.
But what will you feed yourself?

Go wash your hands, go wash
your whole body. Let steam unstiffen
you, the foam drag away the rot.

And after you've combed your hair,
and rubbed sandalwood on your neck,
face the dark ground and kneel,
rest your forehead on the floor.

Say now the alkaline words of forgiveness,
and yes, go ahead and weep out the blows
you've received and recklessly thrown
until supplication is all that pegs you to life.

And when you rise, know that you are not
worthy of disdain or affection, but that
from now on you'll have to tighten your fists
on the last embers of love.

III.

ADULTHOOD

There are boats out there
loading bananas, scrap yard workers
taking down tankers one inch at a time—
the sun over the Indian Ocean,
the blinding glimmer of the sea.

What if one were to walk
toward it, or on it, that call,
that wind blowing between my ribs?

There are weavers,
bolts of damask and rayon,
buttons stitched, and visions lost, grains
of sand falling from their eyes.
Kidneys sold.

Why must you bring me
the same question? A throat being slit,
my hand on the killing hand
guiding it,
the sweet warmth joining us.

Someone is still calling from beyond
the glimmer that drowns my eyes.
Not my angel, not my death,
something closer
that knows what I'll do next.

NIGHT OF THE DULCIMER

For the jailbirds of The Black Horse Prison, Tripoli

The dulcimer player conjures a rankled sea.
Seven years like a torn boot tossed overboard.
Ten years thunk like a rusty anchor,
like an empty bucket of paint.
He calls the octopus from its hiding,
waves millions of jellyfish into shore.

❧

Sad pains ring the dulcimer's sad pains,
the cracked skull, the whipped feet
and the little toe popping off,
the bottle the captive forced to sit upon.
Cigarette burns like sea lice flecking off
a beached whale fall off the dulcimer player,
his nails eking sky out of metal, a herd
of sparks hurtling, igniting into flame.

❧

The dulcimer riles the stingray into frenzy.
They sweep the seabed frothing clouds of chalk.
Five years off my shoulder rattle here,
the milk teeth of my misery about to fall,
my burned books, the wife in the balcony
contemplating suicide, contemplating adultery,
and the shamed child hopeless of the prisoner's return.
Moonshine in our glasses; "drink! drink!"
the dulcimer player sings.

❧

We're naked now like arrows in flight, lustful
for the lover and the grape stains on her cheeks,
the beloved of insidious plans, of ambiguous wishes,
more naked than a wing in the scandal of sky.
The dulcimer player tosses sea urchins at our feet,
the sea's bitter apples roll about our feet.
The coral tenacious, assembles, growing
sugar grain by sugar grain. An idea stands
bright and clear, a light tipping the scales in our favor
and we cheer the new seed, the mating,
mother of pearl trembling on the slick dark face
of brine, the sails' longing writhing to the wind's lash.

❧

Now the dulcimer calls on marshland and swamp,
dives into mossy gullets, grabbing melody
from watery throats. He fills the room with the scent
of trees and amber, pricks the roof with rain
and the smoke of squatters' huts, smoke of charcoal
makers, the scent of fugitives, star shadow, nets of algae
fine as silk fuzz, the bubble of its plankton, the wet fur
of its weed crowding our vision, undrowning us, the reeds
brushing salt off our feathers, the sun breaking into
shards covering the waves with the sand of its sleep.

❧

Dulcimer plucked by bird beaks and snake fangs,
by distance between nerve cell and the sting of pain,
we declare you our law, arrow and quill, the sea
now nimble, supple, adhering to our oars' syntax,
our chant traveling through straits like a smuggler,
loosening the continents' choke hold, our hearts
unchaining calcified sighs, undetaining the vanished
dreamer, appearing the living soul disappeared.

WITH THE RÍMAC DOWN BELOW

Could I have seen what I saw
      had my arms some myth
to map their quest for mooring?

What would I have seen, I who loved her reminisces
      in ease of circumstance—
she who hid behind her father when her mother's anger frothed—

my own father blocks the sheikh from beating
his own son for some mischief—the son years later
      becoming an informant—

and she privileged to lie beside her grandmother, say
      the night before Eid,
you and cousins stacked on a big bed, and the coming
from another city and the falling asleep on a warm night
      and being among them
      sweating their familial sweat.

What would I have seen
in that present of child and kin, in a new city
      reeling in disappointments,
in the way of finished worlds—

another child perhaps tucked in to her grandmother's bosom while
      her younger brothers pined.
She'd landed upon sequence, the sundial destroyed
by conquerors who tore a wall shaped like a jigsaw
      so that history is made.

She'd faced the subsequent plateau,
she now the captured princess,
the market full of hawkers, the sheikh years later carrying a flag,
his moccasins worn to his calloused soles.

You remember the son's shame who'd become one of them
shouting discounts on shirts and sneakers.

You remember her shame before a gynecologist:
"I've carried nine bellies,"
                    telling him half the truth.

"When were you born?" a lover now asks,
not after the first time you'd made love.
"Why did you wait so long?" before you answer her, you ask.

She could track her life like a route on a map, freed of choice.
              You recognize this sense of grace,
your words leading you to a rippled tapestry,
                    a sea, passengers streaming up
or down an airport corridor,

and you think of the word "species,"
and you think an arrival that opens up into quietude
when you at last slept and it felt like a prayer
                    not from you, but to you,

the angels swallowing you in the vortex of their restless wings,
a leavening that grew
                    to contentment, to never have questioned time's want,
her hard years taken like a bitter pill,
her night endured.

And what would you have been to me

had you stepped out of your expected relinquishments?
Who would have taken to them—
the king's dilemma prophesied long ago, one foot metaphysical,
the other resting on an alpaca rug woven by virgin hands?

And where to, in this strange city night
reading eyes—whispering Damascene,
scenting *Nilofar,* the waters Levant—,
           your face among the faces, and being read?

Today renders the father years later
foreseeing dread
                    (his son becoming one of them)
that unsurprisingly came to be embossed on airwaves,
on the face of the sea, the potholed roads.

Today renders the granddaughter
unaware she's learning old ways of making bread—
                    that leavening again.

"When were you born?" she asked.
"When did you become so good at explaining your sadness?"

Some things pass, or are passed on,
the girl watching, allowing a form of ocean to sink her,
                    a swath steeped in attention,
as if afraid of some theft foretold.

And you, traveler's wallet in front pocket,
the beggar-children even younger now (one hiding under the next
           booth afraid of the maitre d)
and the guide, a face molded after a goddess in bronze,
a mother, who mentioned her motherhood only once.

Some day a sense of the present will mollify its shortcomings, you hope,
a ferry leading far and back,
            a melding, yes, but with a sacrosanct pitfall:

The girl was never destined to be a chaste offering, but ushered
into frankincense and the body's bogs.
You see yourself in her procession,
the one misstep in the dance you caught.

Nothing to surpass in the blood then,
you who can only call your openness a kind of motherhood,
            a foggy form of reticence,
lives like books exchanged unread.

"When were you born," she asks, and you say
            to what, not when!

The staircase in the hotel in that city swerving
a double cocooning in the winds' image-mirage
mirroring itself in interstellar chirps,
your heartbeat's thrum and hide.

The ache a wave causes another wave
until no damage is foreign, left unquenched.

LULLABY FOR
THE ABORTED CHILD

Night girl,
night girl,
your book is full.
You have drawn
all the pictures.
You have seen off
all the weepers;
someone else now
wears your garland
of sorrows.
Rainbows pinned
your sky in place.
Stars lit your riverbed.
Moons floated
on your lakes
and washed them.
Do you hear
the swallow that
has begun to sing?
Look at the dewed
branches that tilt
sunlight into eyes.
Mirrors stand heavy
with shadows, curtains
soaked with light,
transparent as air.
Let go of us,
dear child.
Let the day,
at last, give us
meaning.

ON THE MASTHEAD

Writing you from the sky again,
the plane a temple of strangers,
sleepers and insomniacs
needling the unwitting air.

I know you are the sea below,
the moon glow leavening the clouds.
I know you are the smoldering core,
the flame spluttering in eternal dark.

I know you are this journey.
You are separation and welding,
this suspension between eternity and dirt.

You are the love I carry with me,
my anger, my despair,
their atoms trailing from my heart.

You are sleep, the dream
that delights and terrorizes,
captivating, unrecountable.

You happen once and forever
like the air I breathe,
was and will be,
the I in you, the you in I.

I grasp you out of emptiness.
Hold fast to me,
dear little god.
I shall not let go of thee.

EAST OF CARTHAGE: AN IDYLL

1.

Look here, Marcus Aurelius, we've come to see
your temple, deluded the guards, crawled through a hole
in the fence. Why your descendent, my guide and friend

has opted for secrecy, I don't know. But I do know
what to call the Africans, passport-less, yellow-eyed
who will ride the boat before me for Naples, they hope.

Here the sea curls its granite lip at them and flings a winter
storm like a cough, or the seadog drops them at Hannibal's
shores, where they'll stand stupefied like his elephants.

What dimension of time will they cross as the Hours loop
tight plastic ropes round their ankles and wrists?
What siren song will the trucks shipping them back

to Ouagadougou drone into their ears? I look at them
loitering, waiting for the second act of their darkness
to fall. I look at the sky shake her dicey fists.

One can be thankful, I suppose, for not being one of them,
and wrap the fabric of that thought around oneself
to keep the cold wind at bay. But what world is this

that makes our lives sufficient even as the horizon's rope
is about to snap, while the sea and sky ache to become
an open-ended road? That's what we're all waiting for,

a moment to peel itself like skin off fruit, and let us in
on its sweetness as we wait, smoking or fondling provisions,
listening to the engine's invocational purr. In an hour

that will dawn and dusk at once, one that will stretch
into days strung like beads on the horizon's throat,
they will ride their tormented ship as the dog star

begins to float on the water, so bright and still,
you'd want to scoop it out in the palm of your hand.

2.

A pair of Roman fists robbed of spear and shield;
the tiles of the tapestries mixed in with popcorn

that slipped from buttery hands, aluminum
wrappers smudged with processed cheese;

countless cigarette butts surround the fallen
columns and beams with a fringe of tarnished foam;

pairs of panties still hot with forbidden passion...

The ruins are not ruined.
                    Without all this garbage
packed, stratified, how else to name our age?

3.

Earlier, I had walked the market of Sabratha, changed
to its people, but like my old city brought back to me.
The petty merchants, all selling the same goods, shouted out
jokes to each other. A Sudanese waiter carried a tray
with a giant pot of green tea with mint. Among the older men,

their heads capped with crimson shennas, I kept seeking
my father's face. An old lust wafted past me when the abaya-clad
women, scented with knock-off Chanel, sashayed by.
The sawdust floors of the shawarma and falafel eateries,
the sandwich maker dabbing the insides of loaves

with spoons of searing harissa, my mouth watering
to a childhood burn. Pyramids of local oranges,
late season pomegranates, radish and turnip bulbs
stacked like billiard balls, and the half carcasses of lambs
as if made of wax and about to melt off their hooks,

the trays of hearts, kidneys, brains and testicles arrayed
in slick arabesques. The hand-woven rugs where
the extinct mouflon thrives, the glittering new aluminum
wares, the blenders, mincers, hairdryers, and toasters,
their cords tentacles drooping from rusty shelves.

It was as if my eyes were painting, not seeing, what I saw,
my memory slowly building the scene until it assembled whole.
What face did my face put on in the midst of transfiguration?
I know what the eyes of the men my age said, settled now
in comfortable middle age, about the life I left behind.

True, I did envy them the asceticism of their grace,
where a given horizon becomes a birthright—to drive or walk
past the same hills all your life, to eat from the same tree
and drink from the well that gave you your name.

4.

Though for centuries the locals broke the statues'
limbs and ground them to make primitive pottery,
enough remains to echo all that has disappeared:

you and the woman leave the towpath, and you brace her
against the trunk of an oak. It's not moonlight, but refractions
from suburban homes trapped under cloud-cover
that make her bronze skin glow among glistening trees.

First, God made love:
              the canopy like the inside of an emerald,
her lips a rush of cochineal. Then a route of evanescence
brought her from Carthage into these living arms, here.

5.

"A nice time," he tells us, how he and four
cousins crossed the desert heading home
on top of three-years' worth of meager pay
(the tarp ballooning, a giant dough) roped to a truck.

Wearing the goggles of the welder he'd hoped
to become, he looked at the sky and wondered "what
those flying, smoke on their tails, thought of us."

Later, deported in a cargo plane, he handed
the Tuareg soldiers one of his fake passports,
and they like "space aliens" (in shabby uniforms,
sunglasses, tribal veils) poured into his face.

As the propellers' hammering calmed to
a shuddering hum, he saw the stars, "hundreds
of them like gnats" swarm Mt. Akakous' peak.

"My next road is the water," he says serving
us tonight, and we promise, if the coffee is good,
to put him on the next boat to the moon
                              shining over Syracuse.

6.

Suddenly I find your descendant's hands leafing through
my chapters, scribbling a note in the margin of my thoughts:

> "How is it," he asks, "that starlight announces the hour;
> how can a song divide desire in two?"

"My flame," I must have written or said, "coated her body
like silk, one kiss spreading threads of lightening

into her pores, until she became a sob, barely lifted by the wind,
and I became mist, the shadow of a statue at the break of dawn."

> To that he responds, "a Platonic echo;" and
> "What will come out of such plasticine love?"

Marcus Aurelius, your descendent knows I'll leave
as I arrive, so empty he gets lost in me.

7.

Two centuries ago, one of my ancestors sat
on one of the communal latrines in mid-morning
and listened to Apuleius's defense. Across from him
on that marble hexagon, sat two other men.
On normal days they'd have talked about the olive harvest,

the feast of Venus coming soon. But today they listen to
the Madaurian's high eloquence studded with jokes,
cracking their own one-liners, shaking their heads in delight.
Away from the hot midday sun and the throngs,

you could say, they had the best seats in the house,
and so they lingered and heard as much as they could
then went about their business. So what if a man marries
an older woman for her money, what impoverished young Roman
in his right mind wouldn't do that? And sure too, if some man

comes to take your inheritance, even if he's your best friend,
even if he takes good care of your mother, you'd be a fool
not to sue him to the Council, even if you'd have to accuse him
falsely of black magic. That's the beauty of it, or rather,

whoever is going to win will have to make us trust beauty,
that things being already right, can be more right, which
is what "beautiful" really means. And what better way,
to take in all this refinement than hearing it in a latrine
where only beauty shields you from the awful stuff of life.

8.

Marcus Aurelius, the men at the shore follow your path
into eternity, though they already see their journey
as a quarrel with circumstance, their lives abscesses feeding

on the universe's hide, tumors in detention camps,
in basement kitchens. Their pockets filled with drachmas,
they'll lift diffident heads and drag feet lead-heavy with shame.

One of them is now driving a taxi in Thessaloniki or Perugia.
With enough of the language to understand direction, he engages
his late night passengers. In the light of the dashboard

they'll entrust him with their secrets. With time, he'll become
a light unto himself, his car a winged chariot of human folly,
and his responses to them saplings nourished in the dark

soil of philosophy. It's the gift of seasons that stray
from the earth, when soul reigns incidental to flesh,
forgiving to no end, a light that has long surpassed itself.

9.

The birds that drew the line to the first distance
remain nameless to me—

creamy white breasts, gold dust around their eyes,
black/brown (dark roast) wings.

The deserts they crossed, the plains east
or north of here fall like sand from my hands.

Um Bsisi, I want to call them, citizens of a protracted destiny,
native and stranger, prodigal and peasant—

admit now, that you're none of these,
that you're not any,
                    or even all of them combined.

10.

Southwest of here is Apuleius's hometown, his inescapable
destination having spent his inheritance on travel and studies.
"Lacking the poverty of the rich," he'd splurged,
a month-long trip to the Olympic games; and openhanded,
he gifted his mentors their daughters' doweries.

Few return to Madaura once gone, and when heading back
shamefaced like him, they'd do as he did, taking
the longest route hoping the journey would never end. Here
in Sabratha, the widow hooked him, or he let her reel him,
and that's how that sordid business happily ended as it began.

I look out toward Madaura, my back to the theater
and the latrines, Madaura birthplace of Augustine, site of
his first schooling—little Augustine holding a satchel of scrolls
and a loaf of bread for the teacher, awakened by his mother,

his tiny feet cold in tiny sandals, his stomach warm
with a barley porridge my grandmother used to make, forced
to slurp it, sweetened with honey from the Atlas, a sprinkling
of cinnamon and crushed almonds from the family farm.

If the world is that sweet and warm, if it is that mothering,
why then this perpetual scene of separation, this turning
out into the cold toward something he knew he'd love?

He lets go of the neighbors' boy's hand warming his own.
He refuses the warm porridge forever, renounces
his mother's embrace. It only lasted a month,

this partial answer, because even then everyone knew
that the sweet fruit they grew housed the bitterest seeds,
that piety is its own reward while belief only darkens

and deepens like the sea before them, a place
meant for those seeking life other than on this dry earth.
That's why prophets were welcomed here, calmly,
because God was like rain and they like the saplings

which know only the first verse to the sky's rainless hymn.
And that's why Africa's tallest minaret looms unfinished,
visible from the next town over, and for fifty leagues from the sea if
it were turned into a lighthouse for the ships that no longer come.

The merchant who'd built it, money made from smuggling
subsidized goods to Carthage and used Renaults from Rotterdam,
ran out of money, could not afford the mosque that was to stand
next to it, leaving its gray concrete bleaching in the sun.
There's enough history here to enable anyone to finish the thought.

It's useless then to track the fate of these travelers,
some, without life jackets, had never learned how to swim.
Why not let them live in text as they do in life?—they've lived
without words for so long—why not release them
from the pen's anchor and let them drift to their completion?

11.

In a few weeks you'll see pedants here with binoculars
trying to catch a glimpse of the Ramadan crescent,
and if these migrants stick around here
time will belong to the departure of other travelers,

flocks of *Um Bsisi* following the sun's arch,
Japanese and Korean trawlers sailing to Gibraltar
or Suez chasing the last herring or sardine.

Where is she now in her time?—
her life dissolved in other people's minutes,
a sense of solitude her diligent companion
even when she lets go of herself to kindness.

He'll be there when she returns from the party,
he'll lie beside her when she sleeps. He'll say,
"Time belongs to the species, but your life belongs to me."

She'll laugh at his words, and remember what you,
Marcus Aurelius, had said about losing only the moment
at hand, how it circles in a ring of dead nerves,
how we stand impoverished before what is to come.

She'll have her answer to your elocution;
she'd always had an answer for you,
one she refuses to share even with herself.

12.

At last they set to sail. They slaughter a rooster,
douse blood on the Dido figurehead adorning the prow.
The seadog opens a canvas bag and pulls out a hookah.
His Egyptian assistant fills the smoke chamber with seawater,

twists the brass head into it, caking the slit with sand.
He fills the clay bowl with apple-flavored tobacco,
wraps it with foil, pokes it tenderly with a knife.
He picks embers from the going fire, places a few

on the aluminum crown, and inhales and blows
until the bottom vessel fills with a pearly fog,
the color of semen, I think, then hands the pipe hose
to the seadog who inhales his fill and hands it over

to the travelers in turn. The air smells sweet around us,
the breeze blows it away and brings it back tinged with iodine.
Their communion done, they embark except the one who
stands, the dead rooster in his hand, as if wanting

to entrust it to us, then digs a hurried hole to bury it in.
The boat, barely visible, leaves a leaden lacey ribbon
aiming directly for the burnt orange sun. As it reddens,
for a moment, their standing silhouettes eclipse it.

Then the sea restores its dominion, dark as the coffee cooling
in our cups. Dangling from the vine arbor, the lights reflect
a constellation on the table's dark top. I trace my fingers among them,
hoping conjecture would shine on the mind's calculus.

Between my unquiet eddies, Marcus Aurelius,
and the coursing water, the travelers' moment sails,
its tentacles sewing a rupture I had nursed for too long.

POEM

While the light shines and as the breeze rouses
the branches and makes the wind-chimes swoon,
what else can I do but love what casts a shadow
        and bears bulk,
shadow that darkens the bottom of the pond,
that resounds with the equanimity of stone,
        of time running in place,
the petals of a flower waiting for a knock on their door.
I must become as patient as water—
I almost said, I must have become
        a patient of water—,
knowing who I am even as I change,
knowing what ails me as it keeps me sated,
as the earth's pull drags me,
as the sun shuns me or rends me.
I am the pine's stubborn blood.
I am the wind that blows at my back,
        that the wind will tire,
and I will spin away from what passes through me,
that a voice will stand below a window
        and softly sing my name,
a sound, a bay, a whole ocean.
Having all the time in the world,
what else can I do but love what fades?
Having seen it gone and having seen it return,
what else can I do but see to the elements
        in your blood and skin?
Having not felt justified,
having seen so much of the sun's work,
its coyness, its obstinate reach . . .
        I've started a fire,

sat in the poinciana's shade.
Night changes things,
          there's no other way to say it.
What else to do but wait for night to change me?
Having chosen silence to ordain me,
not even thunder could shake its words before me.
Having heard my limbs conspire,
          having heard their vows,
what else can I do but love the shadow that persists,
          that makes things stand still?
Having become a question,
having befriended my sadness,
          what can love do to me now,
but be a reminiscence,
standing below her window,
          my life a sound,
the first vowel of a cautionary tale?
Having seen and having heard, desires mutating
          old new to old,
having the one bed, the one window,
the same letter I write to everyone,
having broken through chains and grammars,
          and your sweet arms,
your hair smelling of coconut, the bitter mud of henna,
your hands smooth, warming my skin,
having now ascended, what else to do but love
          the shadow that extends below?

Amorisco—The title of this volume is a nonce word that combines the Spanish "amor" and "Morisco." Moriscos were Iberian Muslims (Moors) who in the 15th to the 17th centuries were given the choice to convert to Catholicism or leave Iberia. Most were expelled by the decree of 1610 to North Africa and other Muslim territories after being persecuted by the Spanish Inquisition.

"Against Ether"—Francis Bacon: "If a man will begin with certainties, hee shall end in doubts." Thanks to G. W. for the suggestion.

"Before Huron"—The Canaanite referred to in the poem is Ibrahim (Abraham):

> So also did We show Ibrahim the power and the laws of the heavens
>   and the earth so he might, with understanding, have certitude.
> When the night grew dark upon him he saw a star. He said: 'This is
>   my Lord.
> But when it set, he said: I do not love things that set.'
> When he saw the moon rising in splendor, he said: 'This is my Lord.'
> But when the moon set, he said: 'unless my Lord guide me, I shall
>   surely stray.'
> When he saw the sun rising in glory, he said: 'This is my Lord; this
>   is the greatest of all.'
> But when the sun set, he said:
> "O my people! I am indeed free from your guilt of giving partners
>   to God.
> For I have set my face, firmly and truly, towards Him who created the
>   heavens and the earth, and never shall I give partners unto Him."
> —*The Quran* 6:75-79.

The poem also refers to the following passage from *The Quran:*

> "And the Moon, We have measured for him mansions to roam among
>   till he turns like an old and withered date palm frond." (36:39)

"Heartsong"—"The Bedouin pondering the abandoned campsite." The pre-Islamic poetry of Arabia often begins with a nasib wherein the poet meditates upon a site of ruins, such as an abandoned campsite, where his beloved used to live.

The last line of the poem references a line from an untitled poem by Jalaludin Rumi, translated by Kabir Helminski.

"The Old House with Thee"—"Post-Wall" as in post-Berlin Wall.

"Buster"—The line "a pair of parentheses filling in with all that whizzes past" references "Ihtifa bil-Tifula" ("Celebrating Childhood"), a poem by the Syrian poet Adonis.

Christopher Smart, English poet (1722-1771). In the 1750s Smart developed a form of religious mania that made him engage in continuous prayer. Samuel Johnson remarks in Boswell's biography, "My poor friend Smart showed the disturbance of his mind by falling upon his knees, and saying his prayers in the street, or in any other unusual place." The poem alludes to Smart's "For I will consider my cat Jeoffrey" from *Jubilate Agno* (1762), lines 695-742.

"The prestige of a interesting pathology" is from Theodor Adorno's *Minima Moralia*.

"Which"—The poem references "Lebanon is a piece of sky spread on the ground," a line from a song by the Lebanese master Wadii Al-Saafi.

"The In-Between"—"The city of massacred Jewelers" refers to Pforzheim, Germany which was famed for its Jewish jewelers, most of whom perished in the Holocaust.

"Redress"—The last two lines reference a hadith (a saying) by the Prophet Muhammad. "There will come a time when keeping one's faith will be like holding embers in one's hands."

"Night of the Dulcimer"—The dulcimer referred to in the poem is the *qanun,* which is really a zither. The translation here errs on the side of poetry rather than fact. The Black Horse Prison once stood in Tripoli, Libya, and was used by successive regimes for at least six decades to house political prisoners. It was destroyed in 1988. A more modern and more brutal prison, Busleem, has replaced the Black Horse. In an uprising in 1995, the guards at Busleem killed an estimated 1,200 prisoners and buried them on prison grounds. The deaths have never been acknowledged though the government has made attempts to offer small compensations to the victims' families. Attempting to appear the living soul disappeared, the poem celebrates my friends in Libya who survived the Black Horse and Busleem and whose attachment to life and its joy is inspiring and infectious. Since I wrote the poem, I have begun to think of it also as Hisham's poem whose father was detained in Busleem in 1991 and whose fate remains unknown.

"With the Rímac Down Below"—The Rímac River is located in western Peru and is the most important source of portable water for the Lima metropolitan area. "Lima" is a Spanish mispronunciation of the river's Inca name. Nilofar, nenuphar, a white or yellow water-lily native to the southern Mediterranean.

"East of Carthage: An Idyll"—According to various estimates, between 65,000 and 120,000 sub-Saharan and East Africans, as well as South Asians, annually travel to North Africa, crossing the desert on ancient trade routes or via airlines in the hope of reaching Europe. Seventy to 80 percent of them attempt to migrate to Europe from Libyan ports on generally shabby fishing or inflated boats. These transit-migrants sail toward Malta or the Italian islands of Lampedusa, Pantalleria, and Sicily. Most are caught or drown on the journey.

Sabratha, a point of departure of some of these dangerous journeys, is a former Roman colony that lies on the West side of Libya's Mediterranean shore. The city's ruins are among the world's best and most preserved Roman sites and the city was recognized as a World Heritage Site by the United Nations. Marcus Aurelius once visited Sabratha during his reign as emperor while the city was at its cultural and commercial peak. The city built a temple in his honor next to its magnificent Roman theatre, which still stands and is sometimes used for cultural events.

Marcus Aurelius (121-180 A.D.), the Roman emperor who was devoted to Stoic philosophy, perhaps needs no introduction. The poem celebrates his connection to Sabratha and his lingering presence in North Africa where several buildings and monuments are dedicated to him. Inspired by a return to my native Libya after a long absence, the poem also attempts to engage Aurelius's *Meditations,* the classic work of Stoic philosophy in which I found a relevant existential framework for understanding the region and its people.

Apuleius, (123/5-180 A.D.) is the author of *Aureus Asinus, (The Golden Ass)* and a contemporary of Marcus Aurelius. He was born in Maudaura (now Mdaourouch in Algeria). He wrote his *Apologia (A Discourse on Magic)* in Sabratha as his defense against the accusation leveled at him by his best friend and step-son that he had practiced magic.

Section 1 borrows the phrase "granite lip" from Emily Dickinson. Section 4 borrows "A Route of Evanescence" also from Dickinson.

In section 8, *Um Bsisi* is a species of swallows native to Libya. Prevalent in Libyan folklore, *Um Bsisi's* story is emblematic of endless travails.

The poem is for Ashur Etwebi, a descendent of Marcus Aurelius, and native of Sabratha!

"Poem"—Edward Said: "So sufficient is this all-enveloping shadow that one can rest entirely within it, away from any of the common rational forms of human hope or regret."

ACKNOWLEDGMENTS

I am grateful to the 2006-07 fellows of the University of Michigan's Humanities Institute for their generous feedback and support. Thanks also to Danny Herwitz and the rest of the team at the institute for all their help during my fellowship there. Special thanks go to Patsy Yaeger and Kristi Merrill. Iman Mersal and Linda Gregerson combed through the manuscript and offered numerous helpful suggestions. I thank them deeply for their time and thought. Extra-special thanks to Gillian White. To David Wojahn I owe an endless debt of gratitude for years of encouragement and insight, and now for his immense architectural gifts.

Also, I'd like to thank the editors and staff of the following journals for publishing these poems:

American Literary Review: "Adulthood."
Baltimore Review: "Rain-Puddle Birds Bathe at Dawn."
Blackbird: "The Old House with Thee."
Bat City Review: "Adolescence of Burnt Hands" and "Early Adulthood."
Borderlands: "Childhood Fridays."
Crazyhorse: "Corpus Christi."
Hotel Amerika: "The In-Between."
Hunger Mountain: "East of Carthage," sections 2, 6, 10.
Image: "Bedtime Reading for the Unborn Child" and "Lullaby for the Aborted Child."
The Kenyon Review: "Buster."
Margie: "In Praise of Praise."
The Michigan Quarterly Review: "On the Masthead" and "Pastoral."
The Missouri Review: "East of Carthage," sections 1, 3, 7, 9.
Notre Dame Review: "Before Huron."
Packingtown Review: "Night of the Dulcimer."
Ploughshares: "Heartsong."
Prairie Schooner: "With the Rímac Down Below" and "Poem."
Salt Hill: "Which."
Soundings (U.K.): "Night of the Dulcimer."
Third Coast: "Against Ether."
TriQuarterly: "The Violet Bends to the Stubble Skirting It."
Wasafiri: "East of Carthage," section 1, 4, 10, 12.
"Heartsong" also appeared in *Best American Poetry,* 1997 (edited by
        James Tate).

green press
INITIATIVE

Ausable Press is committed to preserving ancient forests and natural resources. We elected to print this title on 30% post consumer recycled paper, processed chlorine free. As a result, for this printing, we have saved:

1 Trees (40' tall and 6-8" diameter)
486 Gallons of Wastewater
1 million BTU's of Total Energy
62 Pounds of Solid Waste
117 Pounds of Greenhouse Gases

Ausable Press made this paper choice because our printer, Thomson-Shore, Inc., is a member of Green Press Initiative, a nonprofit program dedicated to supporting authors, publishers, and suppliers in their efforts to reduce their use of fiber obtained from endangered forests.

For more information, visit www.greenpressinitiative.org

Environmental impact estimates were made using the Environmental Defense Paper Calculator. For more information visit: www.papercalculator.org.